AUSTRALIA & NEW ZEALAND CRUISE GUIDE 2025

A Journey Through Historic Ports, Majestic Coastlines, and Unforgettable Adventures

LARRY B. CARROLL

COPYRIGHT

TABLE OF CONTENTS

INTRODUCTION: WHY CRUISE TO AUSTRALIA & NEW ZEALAND?

Cruising to Australia and New Zealand is more than just a vacation—it's an immersive journey through some of the most stunning and diverse landscapes on Earth. Whether you're looking for golden beaches, dramatic coastlines, vibrant cities, or the thrill of exploring remote wilderness areas, this part of the world has it all. With every stop along the way, the adventure deepens, offering you an opportunity to experience rich cultures, fascinating wildlife, and remarkable natural wonders that can only be fully appreciated from the deck of a cruise ship.

In this guide, we'll dive into why these two countries have become such sought-after cruise destinations. From the vibrant cosmopolitan cities like Sydney and Auckland to the quiet, awe-inspiring fjords and rainforests of New Zealand, Australia and New Zealand offer a unique blend of modern attractions and untamed nature. Whether you're a seasoned cruiser or a first-time traveler, this cruise promises to be an unforgettable experience.

The Unique Allure of Australia & New Zealand

What makes Australia and New Zealand such perfect cruise destinations? The answer lies in their combination of accessibility, variety, and natural beauty. By cruising, you're able to see and experience a broad spectrum of highlights across both countries—often in a way that would be impossible to achieve with a land-based vacation.

Australia is a land of contrasts, offering everything from bustling metropolises like Sydney and Melbourne to the vast, arid landscapes of the Outback. The Great Barrier Reef, one of the world's greatest natural wonders, beckons those with a passion for marine life, while the city streets pulse with a blend of European and native influences. On the other hand, **New Zealand** captivates visitors with its breathtaking fjords, dramatic mountains, geothermal wonders, and rich Maori culture. The diversity of both countries makes them an ideal destination for cruise travelers looking to explore multiple facets of the world in one journey.

Cruising offers a chance to visit multiple cities and regions with minimal stress. From the moment you step onboard your cruise ship, you can relax and enjoy your vacation, knowing that your next exciting stop is just a few days away. No need to worry about packing and unpacking every time you head to a new destination or stress about finding accommodations and transport. Your cruise ship serves as your floating hotel, taking you to the highlights of both countries while you unwind in comfort.

Convenience and Comfort

One of the greatest reasons to consider a cruise in Australia and New Zealand is the unmatched convenience. Cruises offer a comfortable and luxurious way to experience these countries without having to navigate long-haul flights between cities. Your ship becomes a hotel, restaurant, and transportation system all rolled into one, allowing you to see and do much more without the usual travel hassle. From your ship's deck, you'll have an ever-changing view of the coastline, with every port offering a new adventure.

Australia and New Zealand are vast, and their top destinations aren't always easy to access from land. With cruising, you'll get to see more of both countries in less time, and with greater ease. A well-planned itinerary can take you from iconic coastal cities like Sydney to the quieter, pristine shores of New Zealand's North and South Islands, all without stepping foot on an airplane. Your travel is seamless and stress-free, giving you more time to enjoy the wonders of this magical region.

A Perfect Blend of Nature and Culture

Australia and New Zealand are known for their rich history, diverse cultures, and deep ties to the land. New Zealand's indigenous Maori culture is a major draw, offering travelers the chance to learn about their ancient traditions and practices, while

Australia's vibrant Aboriginal culture provides an equally enriching experience.

At the same time, these countries are home to some of the most spectacular natural environments in the world. Whether you're diving into the turquoise waters of the Great Barrier Reef, exploring the ancient rainforests of New Zealand, or cruising past stunning coastal cliffs, the connection to nature is undeniable.

The cities themselves are cultural hubs, offering a blend of modern sophistication and history. In Australia, Sydney's Opera House and Melbourne's street art give a taste of urban elegance, while New Zealand's capital, Wellington, is known for its artistic flair and the world-renowned Te Papa Museum. On a cruise, you'll have ample opportunities to explore both the urban and the wild, ensuring that no part of this extraordinary region is left unexplored.

Variety of Cruise Options

Whether you're looking for a luxury experience with fine dining, entertainment, and every amenity under the sun, or prefer a more laid-back, casual cruise with a focus on relaxation and adventure, Australia and New Zealand have cruise options to suit every style and budget. From all-inclusive, five-star cruise lines to more affordable, family-friendly options, you'll find plenty of ways to make your dream cruise a reality.

Cruise itineraries vary greatly depending on the time of year and the length of your trip, with both short and long-duration cruises available. Many cruises combine stops in both Australia and New Zealand, giving you the chance to experience both countries in one trip. Some cruises even venture into the Pacific Islands, creating the perfect extended vacation for those who want to see as much of the South Pacific as possible.

Making the Most of Your Cruise Experience

Cruising in Australia and New Zealand is all about enjoying the journey, not just the destination. Onboard experiences vary, with many ships offering luxury spas, world-class restaurants, and unique activities to keep you entertained as you travel between ports. From the deck, you can watch the changing landscapes unfold, whether it's a sunrise over the Australian Outback or a sunset in the waters surrounding New Zealand's fjords.

On shore, you'll have plenty of opportunities to engage in exciting activities, from exploring vibrant cities to going on wildlife adventures or indulging in local delicacies. Whether you're taking a scenic helicopter ride over the Great Barrier Reef, enjoying a wine-tasting tour in the Barossa Valley, or hiking through New Zealand's national parks, each port offers something new to discover.

For those looking to enhance their experience, shore excursions can be tailored to your interests, whether you're an adventurer, culture enthusiast, or a foodie. Your cruise line will offer a range of excursions that ensure you get the most out of each stop, with local guides who will provide expert insights into the region's history, culture, and wildlife.

CHAPTER 1: BEST TIME TO CRUISE DOWN UNDER

When it comes to planning your cruise to Australia and New Zealand, timing is everything. Choosing the right season can dramatically impact your experience, from weather conditions to the types of activities available at each port. Understanding when to visit, what to expect weather-wise, and how to pack for different conditions will ensure you have the best possible cruise experience.

In this chapter, we'll explore the peak and off-peak seasons, the weather conditions for each time of year, and what you'll need to pack based on the season. By the end of this chapter, you'll know exactly when to set sail and how to prepare for the unforgettable adventure ahead.

Overview of Peak and Off-Peak Seasons

Australia and New Zealand are both Southern Hemisphere countries, which means their seasons are opposite to those in the Northern Hemisphere. While Europe and North America experience their summer months between June and August, Australia and New Zealand's summer falls from December to February. Understanding these seasonal differences is key when planning your cruise.

Peak Season (December – February)

The peak season in Australia and New

Zealand is during their summer months, which correspond to the holiday season in the Northern Hemisphere. This is when both countries see the highest number of visitors, and for good reason. The weather is warm, the skies are clear, and many major events and festivals take place.

Australia: Sydney hosts the world-famous New Year's Eve fireworks display, and the Great Barrier Reef is perfect for diving and snorkeling. Melbourne, Brisbane, and other cities are bustling with activity during this time, with plenty of outdoor events, festivals, and open-air markets to enjoy.

New Zealand: The weather in New Zealand during summer is perfect for outdoor exploration. This is the best time to visit the North Island's stunning beaches or head to the South Island for hiking in places like Fiordland National Park. The vibrant cities of Auckland, Wellington, and Christchurch also come alive during this period with cultural festivals and outdoor activities.

Off-Peak Season (March – November)
The off-peak season in Australia and New Zealand is from late autumn to early spring (March to November). During this period, the weather can be cooler, and there's less tourist traffic. This makes it a great time for those looking for a quieter, more relaxed experience. While there may be occasional rain or cooler temperatures, this season still offers some incredible opportunities.

Australia: While the summer heat may have subsided, Australia's climate remains warm enough to enjoy coastal cities like Perth, Adelaide, and Sydney. You'll find fewer tourists, which means less crowded beaches and a more laid-back atmosphere at major attractions.

New Zealand: Autumn and spring in New Zealand can be a fantastic time to visit for those who want to avoid the crowds. While the weather can be a bit unpredictable (with chilly mornings and cooler evenings), the crisp air and changing leaves make for a stunning experience. This is an excellent time to explore the South Island's majestic mountains and vineyards without the summer crowds.

Should You Cruise in the Off-Peak Season?

Cruising during the off-peak season has its advantages. With fewer tourists, you'll have a more intimate, less crowded experience. Plus, cruise prices tend to be lower during this time, which is a significant perk for travelers on a budget. However, you'll need to be prepared for slightly less predictable weather, as well as occasional closures or altered schedules due to the offseason.

Weather and Climate Considerations for Each Season

Australia and New Zealand's weather varies significantly depending on where you are. Australia, being a vast country, has a wide range of climates, from the tropical conditions of Queensland to the temperate climate of Tasmania. New Zealand's weather, while more consistent, can still be quite variable, especially in mountainous regions. Understanding these differences will help you pack accordingly and ensure you're comfortable throughout your journey.

Summer (December – February)

Australia: Summer in Australia is hot, particularly in the northern regions, where temperatures can exceed 30°C (86°F) in cities like Brisbane and Cairns. The southern parts, including Melbourne and Sydney, enjoy milder temperatures ranging from 20°C to 25°C (68°F to 77°F). The humidity can be high in places like Darwin and the Great Barrier Reef, while the coastal areas experience more pleasant breezes.

New Zealand: New Zealand's summer is warm but not overly hot, with temperatures ranging from 20°C to 30°C (68°F to 86°F), especially on the North Island. The South Island can be cooler, particularly in the mountainous areas. This is the best time to visit for outdoor activities, as you'll experience long, sunny days perfect for hiking, beach outings, and exploring the cities.

Autumn (March – May)

Australia: Autumn brings cooler temperatures to Australia, but it remains mild and pleasant throughout the country. In the southern regions, the weather can range from 16°C to 23°C (61°F to 73°F). The northern regions like Queensland remain relatively warm, while Melbourne and Sydney experience more moderate temperatures.

New Zealand: Autumn in New Zealand is a spectacular time to visit, with temperatures ranging from 15°C to 22°C (59°F to 72°F). The season offers beautiful foliage, particularly in the central and southern parts of the country. Expect cooler evenings, particularly in the South Island.

Winter (June – August)

Australia: Winter in Australia is relatively mild, with southern cities like Melbourne and Sydney experiencing temperatures around 10°C to 15°C (50°F to 59°F). Northern Australia, including cities like Cairns and Darwin, remains warm, with temperatures around 20°C to 25°C (68°F to 77°F). This is a great time to visit the Great Barrier Reef and Northern Queensland, as it is dry season with little rainfall.

New Zealand: New Zealand's winter is colder, particularly in the South Island, where temperatures often drop below 0°C (32°F) in mountainous areas. The North Island tends to be milder, with temperatures averaging 10°C to 15°C (50°F to 59°F). This is the perfect season for ski enthusiasts who wish to visit places like Queenstown or the Tongariro National Park.

Spring (September – November)

Australia: Spring is one of the most pleasant times to visit Australia. The weather is warm, but not too hot, with temperatures ranging from 18°C to 25°C (64°F to 77°F). It's an excellent time for outdoor activities, as the landscapes come to life with blooming flowers, particularly in places like the Blue Mountains and the coastal regions.

New Zealand: Spring brings a temperate climate to New Zealand, with temperatures ranging from 12°C to 20°C (54°F to 68°F).

The weather can be a little unpredictable, with occasional rain showers, but it's also a time of beautiful blossoms and rejuvenation. The South Island remains cooler, while the North Island is warm and welcoming.

Packing for Summer (December – February)

Clothing: Lightweight and breathable fabrics like cotton, linen, and moisture-wicking materials are essential. Pack plenty of sunscreen, sunglasses, and hats to protect yourself from the sun. Swimsuits, flip-flops, and casual clothing will serve you well for beach days and outdoor excursions.

Layering: Even though it's summer, temperatures can fluctuate, particularly if you're traveling to different regions. Bring a light jacket or sweater for cooler evenings, especially in New Zealand's South Island.

Packing for Autumn (March – May)

Clothing: This is a transition period, so pack layers. Think long-sleeve shirts, sweaters, light jackets, and comfortable shoes. A waterproof jacket or an umbrella will be helpful in case of occasional rain showers.

Accessories: Don't forget a scarf or gloves if you're heading into the mountains or cooler southern regions.

Packing for Winter (June – August)

Clothing: For cooler weather, bring a warm jacket, hat, gloves, and scarves. If you're heading to New Zealand's South Island for skiing or snow activities, make sure to pack thermal wear, a heavy coat, and snow boots.

Footwear: Comfortable, weather-resistant shoes are a must for walking tours, particularly in the colder months.

Packing for Spring (September – November)

Clothing: Similar to autumn, layering is key. Pack light jackets, cardigans, and sweaters for cool mornings and evenings, and lighter clothing for daytime. Waterproof gear is a good idea for the occasional spring rain.

Footwear: Comfortable walking shoes are essential, especially if you plan on exploring outdoor parks or taking scenic tours.

CHAPTER 2: TOP CRUISE PORTS IN AUSTRALIA

Australia is a land of contrasts, with its vast landscapes, bustling cities, and stunning natural wonders. When cruising around Australia, you'll find that each port has something unique to offer, from world-renowned cultural attractions to remote coastal beauty. In this chapter, we'll explore the top cruise ports in Australia, each one providing a different experience and a glimpse into what makes this country so special. Whether you're seeking city excitement, beach relaxation, or adventure in nature, Australia's cruise ports have it all.

Sydney, the largest city in Australia, is known for its iconic harbor, world-class beaches, and vibrant city life. As the first stop on many Australian cruises, Sydney is a bustling metropolis that offers a perfect mix of urban sophistication and natural beauty.

Top Attractions

Sydney Opera House: One of the most famous landmarks in the world, the Opera House is an architectural masterpiece. You can admire its sails from the harbor, take a guided tour, or even catch a world-class performance.

Sydney Harbour Bridge: Climbing this world-famous bridge offers stunning panoramic views of the city and harbor. If you're not up for the climb, simply walking across the bridge is a rewarding experience.

Bondi Beach: Known worldwide, Bondi Beach is an iconic surfing destination. It's also perfect for a relaxing day by the water, enjoying the sun, or walking along the coastal path.

The Rocks: This historic area is home to cobblestone streets, markets, cafes, and pubs. It's where Sydney was first settled, making it a must-visit for history buffs.

What   to   Expect
Sydney is a bustling, cosmopolitan city, offering world-class dining, shopping, and entertainment. It's also an excellent

destination for outdoor activities like hiking and surfing. The city's natural beauty, combined with its modern urban vibe, makes it a favorite among cruise passengers. Sydney is a gateway to exploring more of New South Wales, including the stunning Blue Mountains and the Hunter Valley wine region.

Melbourne: A Cultural and Foodie's Paradise

Melbourne is Australia's cultural capital, offering an eclectic mix of arts, food, and history. Known for its thriving laneway cafes, street art, and European-inspired architecture, this city is a haven for foodies, art lovers, and those seeking a more laid-back city experience.

Top Attractions

Federation Square: This lively square in the heart of the city is home to several museums, galleries, and outdoor spaces. It's a great place to explore Melbourne's creative spirit.

Queen Victoria Market: For food lovers, this historic market is a must-visit. It offers fresh produce, gourmet foods, artisan products, and a variety of international cuisines.

Royal Botanic Gardens: A peaceful escape from the hustle and bustle, the Royal Botanic Gardens are one of Melbourne's most beloved outdoor spaces, perfect for a relaxing stroll or picnic.

National Gallery of Victoria (NGV): As the oldest and most visited public art museum in Australia, the NGV is home to an extensive collection of art from around the world, including European, Asian, and Indigenous works.

What   to   Expect

Melbourne is a city where culture thrives at every corner. Known for its coffee culture and boutique dining, it's a great city to explore on foot. The city has a distinct European feel, with a mix of Victorian and modern architecture. Whether you're a foodie, art lover, or simply want to explore Melbourne's eclectic charm, this city offers something for everyone.

Brisbane is Australia's third-largest city and the gateway to some of the country's most stunning natural wonders, including the Great Barrier Reef and Fraser Island. While the city itself is vibrant and modern, it's the surrounding natural beauty that truly draws visitors.

Top Attractions

South Bank: This riverside precinct offers a perfect blend of parks, cultural attractions, and entertainment. The Queensland Art Gallery and Gallery of Modern Art (QAGOMA) are located here, along with a man-made beach for those who want to cool off.

Lone Pine Koala Sanctuary: If you've always wanted to cuddle a koala, this is the place to be. Lone Pine is the world's first koala sanctuary, and it offers opportunities to interact with Australia's native wildlife.

Moreton Island: Located just off the coast of Brisbane, Moreton Island is a popular destination for day trips, offering stunning beaches, sand dunes, and the chance to swim with wild dolphins.

The Great Barrier Reef: Although not directly in Brisbane, the city serves as a launching point for trips to the Great Barrier Reef, one of the seven natural wonders of the world. Snorkeling, diving, and boat tours are available from here.

What to Expect

Brisbane is a laid-back, sunny city with a strong outdoor culture. The temperate climate allows for year-round activities, and its proximity to the Great Barrier Reef makes it an ideal base for marine adventures. Whether you're exploring the city's vibrant arts scene or heading out on an eco-tour, Brisbane provides a diverse range of experiences for cruise passengers.

Adelaide: Wine Lovers' Dream

Adelaide is a hidden gem in Australia, offering a laid-back atmosphere with a focus on food, wine, and outdoor living. The city is known for its world-class vineyards and close proximity to some of Australia's finest wine regions, including the Barossa Valley and McLaren Vale.

Top Attractions

Barossa Valley: Just a short drive from Adelaide, the Barossa Valley is one of Australia's premier wine regions. Known for its Shiraz and other red wines, the valley offers wine tours, tastings, and gourmet dining experiences.

Adelaide Central Market: For foodies, this is the place to be. Adelaide's Central Market offers fresh produce, local delicacies, and international cuisines. It's a fantastic place to explore and sample the best of the region's food scene.

Adelaide Botanic Garden: This stunning garden is located in the heart of the city and offers a tranquil escape with a range of themed gardens and greenhouses.

Glenelg Beach: Just a short tram ride from the city center, Glenelg Beach offers sun, sand, and a relaxed vibe, perfect for an afternoon stroll or swim.

What to Expect
Adelaide is a peaceful, charming city with a strong focus on local produce and wine. The city's food and wine culture are its main attractions, but the proximity to beautiful beaches and nature reserves also makes it a

great stop for those who want to experience the outdoors. For wine lovers and those seeking a more relaxed pace, Adelaide is a dream come true.

Perth: The Beauty of the West Coast

Perth, the capital of Western Australia, is a city that offers a unique combination of city life and natural beauty. Located on the western coast of Australia, Perth is known for its stunning beaches, relaxed lifestyle, and proximity to some of the most remote and untouched wilderness areas in the country.

Top Attractions

Kings Park and Botanic Garden: Offering panoramic views of the city skyline and the

Swan River, Kings Park is one of the world's largest inner-city parks. It's a perfect place for a walk or picnic, with over 3,000 species of plants to admire.

Cottesloe Beach: One of Perth's most iconic beaches, Cottesloe offers beautiful clear waters and golden sands. It's a great spot for swimming, snorkeling, or simply relaxing in the sun.

Fremantle: Just a short ferry ride from Perth, Fremantle is a historic port town with a lively mix of markets, cafes, and cultural attractions. It's a great place to explore on foot and discover its rich history.

The Swan Valley: Located just outside of Perth, the Swan Valley is one of the oldest wine regions in Australia. Known for its wineries, breweries, and local produce, it's a must-visit for food and wine enthusiasts.

What **to** **Expect**

Perth offers a more relaxed, outdoor lifestyle compared to Australia's eastern cities. With beautiful beaches, parks, and nature reserves, it's the perfect destination for those who want to enjoy the great outdoors. The city also boasts a growing cultural scene, with a variety of galleries, museums, and festivals throughout the year.

CHAPTER 3: TOP CRUISE PORTS IN NEW ZEALAND

New Zealand is a country known for its spectacular landscapes, unique wildlife, and rich indigenous culture. Whether you're drawn to its dramatic fjords, pristine beaches, or vibrant cities, New Zealand's cruise ports are some of the most beautiful and diverse in the world. Each city offers a unique experience, providing a mix of natural beauty and fascinating cultural elements that will make your cruise unforgettable. In this chapter, we'll take you through New Zealand's top cruise ports, each one providing a distinct perspective of this beautiful nation.

Auckland: The Vibrant City Surrounded by Water

As New Zealand's largest city, Auckland is often the first stop for cruise passengers arriving in the country. It's a dynamic metropolis known for its diverse culture, world-class dining, and stunning views of the sea. Auckland sits on an isthmus, surrounded by two harbors, which gives it an abundance of beautiful waterfronts, parks, and beaches. This city is a blend of urban sophistication and natural beauty, making it a perfect start to your New Zealand adventure.

Top Attractions

Auckland Harbour Bridge: The iconic Auckland Harbour Bridge offers a thrilling experience for visitors who want to take part in a bridge climb, with panoramic views of the city and its surrounding islands.

Sky Tower: For breathtaking views of the city, head to the Sky Tower, the tallest freestanding structure in the Southern Hemisphere. You can dine at the revolving restaurant or venture out onto the SkyWalk platform for an adrenaline-pumping experience.

Waiheke Island: Just a short ferry ride from Auckland, Waiheke Island is known for its vineyards, olive groves, and stunning beaches. It's the perfect place for a relaxing day of wine-tasting or hiking along coastal trails.

Auckland War Memorial Museum: Located in the Domain, this museum provides an extensive collection of Maori, Pacific Island, and New Zealand history. It's a must-visit for those looking to learn more about the country's cultural and historical heritage.

What to Expect
Auckland is a bustling, cosmopolitan city, yet it's always within reach of nature, thanks to its numerous harbors, parks, and nearby islands. Whether you're into shopping, outdoor adventures, or learning about the

local culture, Auckland offers something for everyone. It's an ideal gateway for travelers looking to explore the rest of New Zealand.

Wellington: Known for Its Natural Beauty and Rich Culture

Wellington, the capital of New Zealand, is a city known for its artistic vibe, natural beauty, and rich cultural scene. Nestled between rolling hills and a stunning harbor, Wellington offers a delightful combination of outdoor exploration, cultural experiences, and sophisticated dining. The city is often described as the "coolest little capital" due to its dynamic energy, diverse culture, and welcoming atmosphere.

Top Attractions

Wellington Cable Car: Take a ride on the famous cable car that climbs up to the Kelburn lookout. The view from the top offers panoramic vistas of the city and its harbor. At the top, you'll find the Botanic Gardens, a perfect spot for a stroll.

Te Papa Museum: The Museum of New Zealand, Te Papa, is one of the country's most renowned cultural institutions. It offers an in-depth look at New Zealand's history, art, and indigenous culture, including exhibits on Maori culture and natural history.

Wellington Botanic Garden: For nature lovers, the Wellington Botanic Garden provides a lush green space to relax and take in the views. It's a great spot for walking, photography, or simply enjoying the serene surroundings.

Weta Workshop Tour: For film enthusiasts, a visit to Weta Workshop is a must. These special effects studio is behind the iconic creations in films like *The Lord of the Rings* and *The Hobbit*. You can take a behind-the-scenes tour to see how they bring these movies to life.

What**to****Expect**
Wellington is a city that feels both sophisticated and relaxed, with a strong focus on the arts and culture. It's smaller than Auckland but packed with things to see

and do. The city's hilly terrain and scenic waterfront make it a visually stunning place to explore, and its lively café culture makes it a favorite for foodies. Wellington is the perfect port for travelers who want to immerse themselves in the country's history and creative spirit.

Christchurch: The Garden City

Christchurch is often called "The Garden City" because of its lush parks, gardens, and outdoor spaces. It is the largest city on the South Island and offers a perfect combination of Victorian heritage and modern developments. Christchurch is the gateway to the beautiful Canterbury region, with its expansive plains, mountains, and access to nearby adventure destinations.

Top Attractions

Botanic Gardens: Christchurch's Botanic Gardens are a must-see, with beautifully manicured gardens set alongside the Avon River. You can take a relaxing punt (a flat-bottomed boat) ride along the river or simply enjoy the peaceful atmosphere of the gardens.

Antarctic Centre: For something unique, the Antarctic Centre offers an immersive experience about New Zealand's role in Antarctic exploration. The center features interactive exhibits and even a simulated Antarctic storm.

Christchurch Tramway: Hop on a historic tram and enjoy a guided tour of the city. The tram takes you through some of Christchurch's most famous spots, offering both a scenic and informative experience.

Port Hills: For panoramic views of Christchurch, head to the Port Hills. You can drive or take the Christchurch Gondola to the top, where you'll get an incredible view of the city, the Canterbury Plains, and the Southern Alps.

What to Expect

Christchurch is a city that seamlessly blends history and nature. It's a place where the beauty of the outdoors meets the charm of a thriving city center. While Christchurch was heavily impacted by the 2011 earthquake, it has since undergone a transformation, with new public spaces, parks, and innovative architecture. The city is a great starting point for exploring the wider South Island, including nearby beaches and mountain ranges.

Dunedin: The Scottish Charm

Dunedin, located on the southeastern coast of the South Island, is known for its Scottish heritage, charming architecture, and rich wildlife. The city's compact layout and historical buildings give it a European feel, while its stunning natural surroundings offer opportunities for outdoor activities and wildlife watching.

Top Attractions

Otago Peninsula: A short drive from Dunedin, the Otago Peninsula is a haven for wildlife. You can visit the famous Larnach Castle, New Zealand's only castle, or take a wildlife tour to see penguins, albatross, and seals.

Dunedin Railway Station: Often regarded as one of the most beautiful railway stations in the world, the Dunedin Railway Station is a must-see. It's an architectural gem with beautiful gardens and a small museum.

Toitu Otago Settlers Museum: For those interested in learning about Dunedin's history, the Otago Settlers Museum offers a fascinating insight into the region's past, from early Maori settlements to European colonization.

Baldwin Street: Known as the steepest street in the world, Baldwin Street is a unique attraction in Dunedin. Visitors often enjoy climbing the street or simply taking photos at the bottom.

What   to   Expect
Dunedin is a city where Scottish heritage and New Zealand's natural beauty collide. It's a place where history comes alive through stunning Victorian and Edwardian architecture, yet the surrounding landscapes are all about wildlife and outdoor adventures. Dunedin is ideal for

nature lovers and those looking for a city with a bit of old-world charm.

Rotorua: Geothermal Wonders and Maori Culture

Rotorua is located in the heart of New Zealand's North Island, known for its geothermal activity, hot springs, and rich Maori culture. It's a place where the earth literally comes alive, with geysers, bubbling mud pools, and natural hot springs, offering an experience unlike any other.

Top Attractions

Te Puia: Te Puia is a geothermal park and cultural center where you can see the famous Pohutu Geyser in action. You'll also learn about Maori traditions, arts, and crafts, and even experience traditional Maori performances.

Rotorua Museum: Housed in a stunning historic building, the Rotorua Museum offers fascinating exhibits on the region's history, including its volcanic activity, Maori culture, and early European settlement.

Wai-O-Tapu Thermal Wonderland: This is one of the most colorful geothermal areas in New Zealand, featuring steaming geysers, bright green pools, and the famous Champagne Pool.

Polynesian Spa: For a relaxing experience, visit the Polynesian Spa, where you can soak in the naturally heated mineral waters with views of Lake Rotorua.

What to Expect

Rotorua is a city of contrasts, with its natural geothermal wonders and deep Maori heritage. The city's vibrant culture, combined with its outdoor beauty, offers a range of activities, from exploring volcanic landscapes to experiencing traditional Maori performances. Rotorua is perfect for travelers looking for a mix of adventure, culture, and relaxation.

CHAPTER 4: THE BEST CRUISE LINES FOR AUSTRALIA & NEW ZEALAND

Cruising to Australia and New Zealand offers an exciting and immersive way to explore these stunning destinations. However, choosing the right cruise line can make all the difference in your experience, depending on your travel preferences, budget, and the kind of onboard amenities and excursions you're seeking. Each cruise line offers its own unique style, itinerary options, and onboard experiences. In this chapter, we'll explore the top cruise lines serving Australia and New Zealand, highlighting what to expect from each one and breaking down the pros and cons to help you make an informed decision.

Carnival Cruise Line: Fun for the Whole Family

Carnival Cruise Line is known for its lively, fun-filled atmosphere and being budget-friendly. While Carnival caters to a wide range of travelers, it's especially popular with families and younger cruisers looking for an exciting, casual vacation experience.

What to Expect

Onboard Entertainment: Carnival is famous for its fun onboard activities, including themed parties, music, comedy shows, and vibrant nightlife. Their "Fun Ships" live up to their name with nonstop entertainment, making it a great choice for families and young couples.

Family-Friendly Features: Carnival offers numerous kid-friendly activities, including kids' clubs, water parks, and family-friendly dining options. The Carnival Dream, for example, features a 24-hour water park and a ropes course, ideal for both kids and adults looking for fun.

Excursions: In Australia and New Zealand, Carnival offers excursions such as scenic bus tours, visits to wildlife sanctuaries, and cultural experiences. While they tend to focus on popular tourist attractions, Carnival's shore excursions are designed to be accessible to a wide range of travelers.

Pros for Different Types of Travelers

Families: With so many kid-friendly activities, from waterslides to kids' clubs, Carnival is perfect for families who want a casual, affordable vacation. The line offers plenty of entertainment for all ages, making it ideal for multigenerational families.

Young Travelers: If you're traveling with friends or as a couple, the fun, party-like atmosphere on Carnival cruises is a huge draw. It's a great option for those seeking lively nightlife and lots of opportunities to socialize.

Cons

Adults Seeking Tranquility: Carnival's focus on fun can sometimes make the atmosphere feel a bit noisy or hectic, especially for those looking for a more laid-back, relaxed cruise experience. It might not be the best choice for adults seeking peace and quiet.

Luxury Seekers: Carnival is more affordable than luxurious, so if you're looking for gourmet dining, spa treatments, or high-end experiences, it may not meet your expectations.

Royal Caribbean International: Adventure and Luxury Combined

Royal Caribbean is one of the most popular cruise lines worldwide, known for its innovative ships, adventurous activities, and a balance of family-friendly options with luxury features. It's a great choice for those looking to combine relaxation with plenty of adventure.

What to Expect

Innovative Ships: Royal Caribbean is renowned for its state-of-the-art ships that feature thrilling activities like rock climbing, ice skating, surfing simulators, ziplining, and even skydiving simulators (on certain ships). Their ships are often referred to as "floating cities" due to their incredible size and range of amenities.

Dining: From casual buffets to fine dining options, Royal Caribbean's food options are diverse. They also offer specialty dining experiences for a more upscale, gourmet experience. Expect high-quality, international cuisine that caters to various dietary needs.

Excursions: Royal Caribbean offers a broad array of shore excursions in Australia and New Zealand, ranging from guided hikes to scenic train journeys. The cruise line focuses on both active adventures (like kayaking or snorkeling) and cultural tours, providing a well-rounded experience for all types of travelers.

Pros for Different Types of Travelers

Adventure Seekers: If you're looking for exciting, adrenaline-pumping activities, Royal Caribbean is the ideal choice. Its fleet is packed with unique features like surf simulators, rock climbing walls, and more, making it a dream come true for adventure enthusiasts.

Families: With a variety of activities for both children and adults, Royal Caribbean is a great choice for families who want to mix relaxation with excitement. The kids' programs are top-notch, and there's something for everyone aboard the ship.

Luxury Travelers: The line offers luxury experiences, including specialty dining, spa treatments, and suites, making it suitable for those who want a more refined experience, with all the excitement Royal Caribbean provides.

Cons

Cost: Royal Caribbean's cruises can be more expensive than others, especially if you're booking a suite or opting for specialty dining and excursions. The extra activities, while fun, often come at an additional cost.

Crowds: Because Royal Caribbean ships are large, they can feel crowded, especially during peak seasons. If you're looking for a more intimate cruising experience, this may not be the best choice.

Princess Cruises: Elegant and Relaxed with a Focus on Scenic Voyages

Princess Cruises is known for its elegant and relaxed cruising experience. It's an excellent choice for those who want to immerse themselves in scenic landscapes, enjoy exceptional service, and indulge in luxury without the frenetic energy of some other cruise lines. Princess is ideal for travelers seeking a serene, refined, and culturally immersive cruise experience.

What to Expect

Scenic Cruising: Princess Cruises is renowned for its scenic itineraries, and in Australia and New Zealand, this includes visits to destinations like the Great Barrier Reef and Fiordland National Park. Their ships offer plenty of opportunities to relax and enjoy the view, with panoramic lounges, large outdoor decks, and excellent observation areas.

Dining: Princess Cruises offers a variety of dining options, from buffets to fine dining. They have a reputation for high-quality meals and offer specialty dining for those seeking a more upscale experience. The line also caters to dietary restrictions with ease.

Onboard Entertainment: While not as flashy as some other cruise lines, Princess Cruises offers live shows, movies, and lectures, providing a more laid-back form of entertainment. The emphasis is on creating a relaxed and refined atmosphere rather than non-stop action.

Pros for Different Types of Travelers

Couples and Honeymooners: If you're looking for a relaxed, romantic cruise experience, Princess Cruises excels. Their focus on scenic cruising and quiet luxury makes it ideal for couples seeking a peaceful vacation.

Mature Travelers: Princess Cruises appeals to older travelers, offering a slower pace with more traditional cruise activities like afternoon tea, enrichment lectures, and wine tastings.

Nature Lovers: With itineraries designed to take you through some of the world's most beautiful natural landscapes, Princess Cruises is perfect for nature enthusiasts. Their ships are equipped with observation decks and panoramic lounges, so you won't miss a single scenic view.

Cons

Limited Adventure: If you're seeking lots of thrills, such as rock climbing, zip-lining, or surfing simulators, Princess might not offer the excitement you're looking for. The line is focused more on relaxed activities and scenic cruising than adventure.

Higher Price Point: While not the most expensive cruise line, Princess can be pricier than budget options. Specialty dining, excursions, and spa treatments all come at an additional cost.

Norwegian Cruise Line (NCL): Flexible and Fun for All Ages

Norwegian Cruise Line (NCL) is known for its "Freestyle Cruising" concept, which offers travelers more flexibility and freedom compared to traditional cruise lines. With a wide variety of dining options, activities, and entertainment, Norwegian is a great choice for those who want a relaxed cruise with plenty of freedom to customize their experience.

What to Expect

Freestyle Cruising: One of Norwegian's defining features is the ability to dine when and where you like, with no set dining times. This makes it an excellent choice for travelers who dislike rigid schedules and prefer a more flexible vacation.

Activities and Entertainment: From Broadway-style shows to themed parties and entertainment, Norwegian Cruise Line is perfect for those seeking a lively atmosphere. Activities like laser tag, ropes courses, and waterslides are also available.

Excursions: In Australia and New Zealand, Norwegian offers a variety of shore excursions that cater to all interests, from wildlife encounters to scenic tours. You can enjoy everything from adventure-packed excursions to cultural experiences and nature tours.

Pros for Different Types of Travelers

Families: With its variety of activities, kid-friendly spaces, and flexible dining options, NCL is ideal for families looking for a fun, casual cruise experience.

Couples: If you're seeking a more relaxed, flexible vacation, NCL's Freestyle Cruising concept allows you to have a laid-back, romantic time without the pressures of formal dining and schedules.

Social Travelers: Norwegian cruises are perfect for socializing and meeting new people. The wide range of activities and entertainment, combined with the flexible dining options, make it easy to mingle and enjoy your vacation on your terms.

Cons

Lack of Structure: While flexibility is a big selling point for many, some travelers might prefer the structure of more traditional cruises with set dining times and activities.

If you like having a clearly defined schedule, NCL's Freestyle Cruising may feel too laid-back.

Cost of Extras: While NCL is generally affordable, some of the onboard activities and excursions can add up, making it a less budget-friendly option for those on a tight budget.

CHAPTER 5: ONBOARD EXPERIENCE: WHAT TO EXPECT

When embarking on a cruise to Australia and New Zealand, the journey itself becomes just as exciting as the destinations. One of the main appeals of cruising is the wide array of onboard experiences, from the dining options to the entertainment and everything in between. Whether you're seeking a culinary adventure, a chance to unwind and relax, or engaging family activities, there's something for everyone on board. In this chapter, we'll explore the various aspects of the onboard experience you can expect when cruising to Australia and New Zealand.

One of the greatest pleasures of cruising is the chance to indulge in a variety of world-class dining options. Cruise lines serving Australia and New Zealand offer an exciting mix of international cuisine with local flavors, giving passengers the opportunity to savor dishes inspired by the destinations they're visiting.

What to Expect

Variety and Quality: Onboard dining usually includes a mix of casual eateries, buffet-style options, and specialty restaurants. Expect to find everything from Italian, French, and Asian cuisines to more traditional Australian and New Zealand fare. You'll likely encounter local ingredients like fresh seafood, lamb, and native produce like Wattleseed and Kakadu plums, which are often incorporated into dishes for a truly authentic experience.

Casual Dining: Most cruise lines offer casual dining options where you can grab a quick bite whenever you want. Expect to find buffet-style dining, where you can sample various international dishes. On some ships, there are also outdoor grills, pizzerias, and cafes offering everything from burgers and pizza to fresh salads and pastries.

Fine Dining: For a more upscale dining experience, specialty restaurants serve refined dishes, often with an emphasis on regional ingredients. Fine dining options might include Australian-inspired steakhouse experiences, seafood platters featuring local catch like barramundi and mud crab, or New Zealand lamb dishes. Many ships also offer wine pairings, allowing you to try wines from Australia's renowned vineyards or New Zealand's world-class wineries.

Room Service: For those who prefer dining in the comfort of their cabin, most cruise lines provide 24-hour room service. You can enjoy your meal while taking in stunning views from your balcony or simply relaxing in your room.

Local Flavors You Might Encounter

Australia: Expect to see dishes inspired by the vast natural bounty of Australia. For instance, you might encounter kangaroo steak, emu, or crocodile, as well as plenty of fresh fish like barramundi and seafood platters.

New Zealand: New Zealand's cuisine often features tender lamb (especially from the South Island), as well as fresh seafood like green-lipped mussels and Bluff oysters. Don't forget to try a classic Kiwi dessert, pavlova, which is a meringue-based dessert topped with fresh fruit.

What to Look For in Australia & New Zealand

Cruise lines often include excursions that incorporate food experiences, like guided tours of local wineries or cooking classes where you can learn how to prepare traditional dishes with local ingredients. This enhances the onboard dining experience and ties in perfectly with your visit to Australia and New Zealand.

Entertainment: Shows, Activities, and Relaxation

A cruise to Australia and New Zealand offers an abundance of entertainment options, both day and night. Whether you're in the mood for a high-energy show, a relaxing spa experience, or an engaging cultural activity, you'll find something to suit your mood.

What to Expect

Live Shows and Performances: Expect top-notch entertainment that may include Broadway-style shows, musicals, live bands, comedy acts, and more. Many cruise lines also feature local performances, such as cultural dances or performances inspired by Australian and Maori heritage. These are designed to give you a taste of the destinations you're visiting while providing an enjoyable evening out.

Activities and Classes: For those looking to stay active or learn something new, onboard activities such as dance classes, cooking demonstrations, and arts and crafts workshops are common. Cruise lines often offer enrichment programs that delve into topics related to your destination, such as Australian wildlife or the history of the Maori people.

Relaxation: Cruises are also about relaxation. Many ships boast luxurious spas where you can enjoy a rejuvenating massage, facial, or thermal therapy experience. If you're looking for something more laid-back, the pools, hot tubs, and lounges offer the perfect environment to unwind, whether you're enjoying a cocktail or simply taking in the views.

Cultural Experiences: You'll also find educational experiences onboard, such as talks and presentations by experts. For example, you might attend a lecture on the history and geography of the Great Barrier Reef, or a talk about New Zealand's indigenous Maori culture and traditions. These experiences help enrich your understanding of the places you're visiting.

Themed Nights and Parties Many cruise lines offer themed parties and events that keep the fun going into the night. These might include:

Aussie BBQ Nights: Featuring Australian specialties like grilled kangaroo or a traditional seafood barbecue.

Maori Cultural Nights: For those cruising to New Zealand, you might enjoy an evening of traditional Maori music, dance, and storytelling.

What   to   Look   For

While larger ships often have a wider variety of entertainment options, even smaller ships offer intimate performances and relaxing onboard experiences. Be sure to check the daily itinerary for shows, parties, and other events happening on the ship so you don't miss out on the fun.

Family-Friendly vs. Adult-Only Experiences

When it comes to onboard experiences, cruise lines offer a wide spectrum of activities, from family-friendly adventures to adult-only zones, so everyone can find a way to enjoy their time aboard. Here's how the two differ:

Family-Friendly Experiences

Kids' Clubs: Most cruise lines offer dedicated kids' clubs that cater to children of all ages. These clubs feature supervised activities such as arts and crafts, sports, video games, and more. Many ships also have special programs designed to teach kids about the wildlife and cultures of Australia and New Zealand, making it both fun and educational.

Family Pools and Water Parks: On family-oriented ships, you can expect pools with slides, splash zones, and even water parks designed for children. Families can enjoy these areas together, allowing parents to relax while kids are entertained.

Family Dining: Many ships offer family-friendly dining experiences, with kid-approved menus featuring a range of options like pizza, pasta, and chicken fingers. Buffets are also great for families, as they provide plenty of choices to satisfy picky eaters.

Adult-Only Experiences

Adult-Only Areas: For those traveling without children, cruise lines often offer adult-only areas, including pools, spas, and even entire decks dedicated to adults. These are perfect for those who want a more serene, peaceful environment without the hustle and bustle of families and children.

Specialty Dining: Many cruise lines feature exclusive, adults-only dining venues where guests can enjoy a refined, more intimate dining experience away from the family crowds. These venues often focus on gourmet cuisine, wine pairings, and a quiet, elegant atmosphere.

Entertainment and Lounges: In addition to family entertainment, there are often lounges, bars, and nightclubs designed specifically for adults. These spots usually feature live music, sophisticated cocktails, and a relaxed, adult-oriented ambiance. On some cruises, you'll also find 18+ comedy shows, theater performances, and themed dance nights designed for an adult audience.

Spa and Wellness: Many cruise lines offer adult-only wellness programs, including spa treatments, yoga classes, and meditation sessions. Some ships even have couples' massages and private spa suites for those looking to unwind together.

What   to   Expect
Cruise lines like Royal Caribbean and Norwegian Cruise Line offer dedicated areas for both family-friendly fun and adult-only relaxation. If you're traveling with both kids and adults, you'll likely experience a balance of activities that cater to everyone's needs. On the other hand, luxury cruise lines or

those like Celebrity Cruises may cater more to adults with upscale dining, entertainment, and spa options, with fewer family-focused activities.

CHAPTER 6: EXPLORING AUSTRALIA & NEW ZEALAND'S TOP ATTRACTIONS

Australia and New Zealand are known for their extraordinary natural beauty, rich cultural history, and unique landmarks. A cruise to these destinations offers more than just stunning ocean views—it's an opportunity to experience some of the world's most iconic sites, both natural and man-made. In this chapter, we'll explore the top attractions in both countries, offering helpful tips for getting the most out of your visit to each one.

The Great Barrier Reef is one of the most famous natural wonders in the world. Stretching over 2,300 kilometers along Australia's northeast coast, this UNESCO World Heritage Site is home to an incredible array of marine life. Whether you're a seasoned diver or a first-time snorkeler, the Great Barrier Reef is an experience like no other.

What to Expect

Diverse Marine Life: The Great Barrier Reef is teeming with vibrant coral formations, colorful fish, sea turtles, and even majestic manta rays. It's one of the best places in the world for underwater exploration.

Clear Waters: Visibility is generally excellent, especially during the summer months, when the water is warm and calm. In some areas, you can see over 30 meters underwater.

Day Trips: Many cruises include shore excursions to reef areas such as Green Island, Fitzroy Island, or the Whitsundays, where you can snorkel or dive. Some excursions offer guided diving experiences for beginners or more advanced divers.

Snorkeling Tips

Choose the Right Spot: Some reef areas are more accessible to beginners, while others require more advanced skills. If you're new to snorkeling, opt for guided tours where you'll be accompanied by experienced instructors. Areas like the Whitsundays are perfect for beginners.

Protect Yourself: The sun can be intense, so always wear a reef-safe sunscreen, a rash guard, and a hat to protect yourself from sunburn. Be mindful of coral when swimming and try not to touch anything, as it can damage delicate ecosystems.

Take a Waterproof Camera: Don't miss the chance to capture the underwater beauty of the reef. Waterproof cameras are perfect for snapping photos of the stunning marine life and crystal-clear waters.

Diving Tips

Certified Divers: If you're already a certified diver, you'll be in for a treat. There are many world-renowned dive sites within the reef, such as the Ribbon Reefs and Osprey Reef. These areas offer an unforgettable experience with diverse marine life, coral gardens, and underwater caves.

Stay Safe: Make sure to dive with a reputable company, always follow safety instructions, and avoid diving if you have any health conditions that could be affected by the underwater pressure.

The Outback is an iconic part of Australia's identity. It's a vast, remote region that stretches across much of the country, filled with rugged landscapes, rich cultural history, and unique wildlife. A visit to the Outback offers a glimpse into the heart of Australia, where nature and history come together in fascinating ways.

What to Expect

Uluru (Ayers Rock): One of Australia's most famous landmarks, Uluru is a massive sandstone monolith located in the Northern Territory. It holds great cultural significance for the local Anangu people. While visiting, you can enjoy walking tours, learn about its Aboriginal history, or watch the sunset as the rock changes color.

Kings Canyon: A stunning natural wonder located in Watarrka National Park, Kings Canyon offers breathtaking views, ancient rock formations, and unique flora and fauna. The Rim Walk is a popular hike that takes you to the top of the canyon, where you can enjoy panoramic views of the surrounding desert.

Alice Springs: This iconic desert town is the perfect base for exploring the Outback. You can visit the Alice Springs Desert Park to learn about the region's unique ecosystems, wildlife, and indigenous culture.

What to Do

Wildlife Watching: The Outback is home to some of Australia's most iconic wildlife, including kangaroos, dingoes, and emus. You can also spot unique birds, reptiles, and desert-dwelling mammals.

Cultural Tours: Aboriginal cultural tours provide insight into the traditions, stories, and history of the Indigenous peoples who have lived in the Outback for thousands of years. These tours often include visits to sacred sites and hands-on experiences with traditional crafts and customs.

Desert Stargazing: The clear desert skies make the Outback an ideal location for stargazing. Many tours offer a chance to view the stars and planets through telescopes while learning about the night sky's significance in Aboriginal culture.

New Zealand's Fiordland: Cruises to the World's Most Stunning Fjords

Fiordland is a region located in the southwestern corner of New Zealand's South Island, renowned for its dramatic fjords, towering cliffs, and lush rainforests. Fiordland National Park is home to some of the most breathtaking landscapes in the world, making it a must-visit destination for nature lovers and those on a cruise to New Zealand.

What to Expect

Milford Sound: Arguably the most famous of New Zealand's fjords, Milford Sound is a breathtaking natural wonder. The fjord is surrounded by steep mountains, cascading waterfalls, and thick rainforest. Cruising through Milford Sound is a bucket-list experience that offers some of the best views in the country.

Doubtful Sound: Known for its more remote and tranquil atmosphere, Doubtful Sound is another stunning fjord in Fiordland. It's less crowded than Milford Sound, making it an excellent choice for those seeking a more peaceful and intimate experience.

Dusky Sound: One of the largest and most isolated fjords in Fiordland, Dusky Sound is known for its wildlife and pristine beauty. It's an excellent destination for birdwatching and cruising, offering a chance to explore the rugged wilderness.

What to Do

Scenic Cruising: Many cruises to Fiordland will take you through these magnificent fjords, offering stunning views from the comfort of your ship. Some tours offer additional activities like kayaking, fishing, or even overnight stays in the fjords.

Hiking: If you prefer to experience the landscape up close, Fiordland offers numerous hiking trails that wind through its rainforests and along its dramatic shorelines. The Routeburn Track is one of the most popular hikes, offering spectacular views of the fjords, mountains, and waterfalls.

Wildlife Spotting: The waters of Fiordland are teeming with wildlife, including dolphins, seals, and penguins. Many cruises offer the opportunity to see these animals in their natural habitat, providing a truly magical experience.

Sydney Opera House and Harbour Bridge: A Must-See in Sydney

Sydney is one of Australia's most iconic cities, and no visit would be complete without experiencing its most famous landmarks: the Sydney Opera House and Sydney Harbour Bridge.

What to Expect

Sydney Opera House: This architectural masterpiece is one of the most recognizable buildings in the world. Take a guided tour to learn about its history, design, and cultural significance. If you have the chance, catch a performance at the Opera House, whether it's a symphony, a play, or a ballet.

Sydney Harbour Bridge: Climbing the Sydney Harbour Bridge offers spectacular views of the city and the harbor. For those not keen on climbing, simply walking across the bridge is an experience in itself, allowing you to take in the beautiful surroundings from above.

What to Do

Opera House Tour: A guided tour of the Opera House will take you behind the scenes and show you the inner workings of this iconic building. You can also catch one of its many performances.

Bridge Climb: If you're feeling adventurous, a Bridge Climb gives you a unique perspective of Sydney's harbor and skyline. The climb is guided, and you'll be equipped with all the necessary safety gear.

Harbour Cruise: For the best views of both the Opera House and Harbour Bridge, consider taking a harbor cruise. These cruises offer a relaxing way to enjoy the sights of Sydney's beautiful harbor.

Māori Culture and Heritage in Rotorua

Rotorua, located on New Zealand's North Island, is not only known for its geothermal activity but also for its deep Māori cultural heritage. Rotorua offers a unique opportunity to immerse yourself in the traditions and customs of New Zealand's indigenous people.

What to Expect

Te Puia: Te Puia is a cultural center and geothermal park where you can experience the traditions and arts of the Māori people. You can witness the famous Pohutu Geyser in action while learning about the significance of Māori culture and history.

Maori Village Experiences: Many local tour operators offer experiences where you can visit traditional Māori villages, watch cultural performances, and participate in ancient rituals like the welcoming "haka" dance.

Wai-O-Tapu: This geothermal wonderland features colorful hot springs, boiling mud pools, and geysers. It's a fantastic place to learn about the volcanic activity that shaped New Zealand's landscape, while also experiencing Māori storytelling and traditions.

What to Do

Cultural Shows and Feasts: Attend a traditional Māori cultural performance followed by a "hangi" feast, where food is cooked in an underground oven. It's a fantastic way to experience the warmth and hospitality of the Māori people.

Geothermal Tours: Rotorua is one of the best places in the world to witness geothermal activity. Take a guided tour to explore the area's geysers, mud pools, and hot springs, while learning about the geological history and Māori legends associated with the region.

CHAPTER 7: SHORE EXCURSIONS: MAXIMIZING YOUR TIME ON LAND

One of the most exciting aspects of a cruise to Australia and New Zealand is the opportunity to explore the diverse cities, landscapes, and cultural landmarks during your shore excursions. With each port offering unique activities and experiences, it's important to maximize your time on land by carefully selecting the best tours, attractions, and experiences. However, it's also essential to be aware of common scams that can target unsuspecting cruisers. In this chapter, we'll explore the must-do activities at each port, recommend tours and excursions in major cities and regions, and provide tips on how to avoid common cruise port scams.

Whether you're exploring vibrant cities, natural wonders, or historical landmarks, there's something for everyone in Australia and New Zealand. Here are some of the best must-do activities for each major port:

Sydney, Australia

Sydney Opera House Tour: This world-famous landmark is a must-see. Take a guided tour to explore the history, architecture, and significance of this iconic building.

Sydney Harbour Bridge Climb: For spectacular panoramic views of the city and harbor, take the thrilling Bridge Climb. The climb is guided and offers a chance to see Sydney from a unique perspective.

Bondi Beach: Spend a day relaxing at one of Sydney's most famous beaches. You can enjoy the sun, surf, and even take a coastal walk to Coogee Beach.

Royal Botanic Garden: Located near the Opera House, this beautiful garden is a peaceful escape in the heart of the city. It's perfect for a relaxing stroll with views of the harbor.

Melbourne, Australia

Federation Square: Explore this cultural hub with its unique architecture, museums, and galleries. It's also home to the Australian

Centre for the Moving Image (ACMI) and the National Gallery of Victoria.

Great Ocean Road Tour: One of Australia's most scenic drives, this tour takes you along the stunning coastline, stopping at landmarks like the Twelve Apostles and Loch Ard Gorge.

Queen Victoria Market: Visit this iconic market for fresh local produce, artisanal goods, and vibrant street food. It's the perfect spot for a relaxed lunch.

Yarra River Cruise: Take a relaxing boat cruise along the Yarra River to get a unique view of Melbourne's skyline and major landmarks.

Brisbane, Australia

Lone Pine Koala Sanctuary: A visit to this sanctuary offers a chance to hold a koala, feed kangaroos, and see other Australian wildlife up close. It's a fantastic family-friendly excursion.

Noosa National Park: This coastal national park is perfect for hiking and enjoying breathtaking views of the ocean, with the chance to spot dolphins and sea turtles.

Story Bridge Adventure Climb: If you're looking for adventure, take a climb up the Story Bridge for incredible views of the city and surrounding areas.

South Bank Parklands: This vibrant area features parks, walking paths, gardens, and a lagoon with a man-made beach, perfect for a relaxing afternoon in Brisbane.

Cairns, Australia (Great Barrier Reef)

Great Barrier Reef Snorkeling/Diving: Whether you're a beginner or an experienced diver, the Great Barrier Reef offers unforgettable underwater experiences. Snorkelers can enjoy shallow waters, while divers can explore deeper, more pristine sites.

Kuranda Scenic Railway and Skyrail: This historic railway journey through the rainforest leads to the village of Kuranda. You can also ride the Skyrail Rainforest Cableway for spectacular views of the tropical rainforest and Barron Gorge.

Daintree Rainforest: Take a tour of one of the oldest rainforests in the world. The Daintree Rainforest is home to diverse wildlife, including the endangered cassowary, and offers plenty of opportunities for nature walks.

Auckland, New Zealand

Sky Tower: Head up to the Sky Tower for panoramic views of the city, the Hauraki Gulf, and the surrounding islands. It's a great spot for photos and offers a chance to see Auckland from above.

Waiheke Island: Just a short ferry ride from Auckland, Waiheke Island is known for its vineyards, olive groves, and beautiful beaches. It's a great place for a wine tour, hiking, or enjoying the local art scene.

Auckland War Memorial Museum: This museum offers fascinating exhibits on New Zealand's history, natural environment, and indigenous Maori culture. It's a great way to learn about the country's heritage.

Wellington, New Zealand

Te Papa Museum: This world-class museum offers extensive exhibits on New Zealand's history, art, and culture. Highlights include Maori artifacts and exhibits on the country's natural environment.

Wellington Cable Car: Ride the famous cable car to the top of the hill for stunning views of the city and harbor. At the top, you'll find the Botanic Gardens, perfect for a relaxing walk.

Wellington's Waterfront: Explore the waterfront with its cafes, restaurants, and cultural sites. It's a lovely area to stroll and take in the sights, especially on a sunny day.

Rotorua, New Zealand

Te Puia Geothermal Park: Visit this geothermal park to see boiling mud pools, geysers, and learn about Maori culture. It's a great way to experience the region's natural wonders and cultural heritage.

Rotorua Lakes: Rotorua is home to several beautiful lakes, including Lake Rotorua and

Lake Taupo. These offer opportunities for boating, fishing, and relaxing by the water.

Maori Cultural Experiences: Attend a traditional Maori performance and feast, where you can learn about the history and customs of New Zealand's indigenous people while enjoying a delicious meal cooked in an underground oven (hangi).

Recommended Tours and Excursions in Major Cities and Regions

Cruise lines typically offer a variety of shore excursions to cater to different interests and activity levels. Whether you prefer a relaxing day on the beach or an adventurous hike, there's something for everyone. Here are some recommended tours for major cities:

Sydney Opera House and Harbour Bridge Combo Tour: Many cruise lines offer a combination tour of the Opera House and Harbour Bridge, giving you the chance to see two of Sydney's most iconic landmarks in one excursion.

Great Barrier Reef Adventure: Several cruise operators offer day trips to the Great Barrier Reef, including guided snorkeling and diving excursions. These tours often include lunch, wetsuit rentals, and expert guides.

Melbourne's Great Ocean Road and Twelve Apostles Tour: This scenic day tour takes you along one of the world's most famous coastal drives, with stops at the Twelve Apostles, Loch Ard Gorge, and other stunning viewpoints.

How to Avoid Common Cruise Port Scams

While shore excursions can be a highlight of your cruise, it's essential to be cautious of common scams that can target cruise passengers in popular ports. Here are some tips to help you avoid falling victim to scams during your time on land:

Be Wary of Overpriced Tours

If you're booking excursions independently (not through the cruise line), make sure to research the company beforehand. Look for reputable tour operators with good reviews to avoid overpriced tours or unreliable services.

Avoid Unlicensed Taxis and Ride Services

When getting off the ship, be cautious of unlicensed taxi drivers or individuals offering "special deals" for tours or rides. Always use registered taxis or reputable ride-sharing services like Uber. Cruise lines typically provide official transportation options.

Beware of Fake Souvenir Sellers

Vendors selling souvenirs in port areas may sometimes offer items at inflated prices. Be cautious of counterfeit goods or items that may not be authentic. It's always a good idea to compare prices with other shops or markets.

Don't Fall for "Too Good to Be True" Deals

If someone offers you an incredible deal on a tour or excursion, especially on the dock or near the port, be cautious. It's always best to research excursions in advance or book through your cruise line for peace of mind.

Keep Your Personal Belongings Secure

Ports can be busy, and crowded areas are often a hotspot for pickpockets. Keep your valuables secure and be mindful of your surroundings. Always carry a small bag or backpack and avoid displaying expensive items like jewelry or cameras.

Check the Fine Print

If booking a tour, ensure that all details are clearly outlined, including the tour's duration, inclusions, and costs. If the deal seems too good to be true, it may have hidden fees.

CHAPTER 8: CLIMATE AND WEATHER CONDITIONS FOR YOUR CRUISE

Understanding the climate and weather conditions in Australia and New Zealand is essential when planning your cruise. The weather can significantly impact your experience on board and your shore excursions, so it's crucial to know what to expect for each season and how it may affect your trip. In this chapter, we'll dive into the average temperatures, seasonal variations, and the best months for cruising each country. We'll also look at how weather can influence cruise schedules and shore excursions, helping you make informed decisions for your cruise to the "Land Down Under."

Australia and New Zealand have diverse climates due to their size and geographical variety. Each region offers a different experience depending on the time of year, and understanding these differences can help you pack appropriately and plan for the type of weather you'll encounter.

Australia

Australia's climate varies dramatically from one region to another, ranging from tropical in the north to temperate and

Mediterranean in the south. Here's what you can expect:

Summer (December to February): Summer is the peak cruising season in Australia, with warm temperatures and longer days.

Sydney: Expect average temperatures between 64°F (18°C) and 79°F (26°C). It can be humid, especially in the northern regions, but it's also the best time to enjoy Sydney's beaches, outdoor activities, and events.

Melbourne: Temperatures range from 59°F (15°C) to 79°F (26°C). Summer in Melbourne is sunny, but it can sometimes be unpredictable, with occasional heatwaves and cooler spells.

Brisbane & Cairns: The tropical north experiences temperatures between 75°F (24°C) and 88°F (31°C). This time of year is ideal for water activities, although rain is possible, especially in Cairns.

Autumn (March to May): Autumn offers more moderate temperatures, making it a pleasant time to cruise.

Sydney: Temperatures cool down a bit to between 57°F (14°C) and 74°F (23°C), making it perfect for outdoor sightseeing and walking around the harbor.

Melbourne: The weather remains mild, with temperatures ranging from 50°F (10°C) to 68°F (20°C). The autumn foliage in

Melbourne's parks and gardens is a highlight.

Brisbane & Cairns: Northern Australia remains warm but comfortable, with temperatures averaging between 70°F (21°C) and 84°F (29°C), ideal for sightseeing and outdoor activities.

Winter (June to August): Winter is off-peak season in Australia, but it's still a good time for cruising if you prefer cooler temperatures and fewer crowds.

Sydney: Winters are mild, with temperatures between 48°F (9°C) and 64°F (18°C), making it a great time to explore the city's landmarks and museums without the intense summer heat.

Melbourne: Winter can get quite chilly, with temperatures between 41°F (5°C) and 57°F (14°C), with occasional rainfall. Pack warm clothing if you're heading here.

Brisbane & Cairns: The tropical north stays relatively warm, ranging from 59°F (15°C) to 75°F (24°C), but it's generally the off-season, meaning fewer tourists and more relaxed vibes.

Spring (September to November): Spring brings pleasant weather across Australia, with mild temperatures and more sunshine.

Sydney: Expect temperatures between 54°F (12°C) and 72°F (22°C). Spring is a wonderful time to visit, with warm days and cooler nights perfect for outdoor exploration.

Melbourne: Spring temperatures range from 50°F (10°C) to 70°F (21°C). It's a great time to visit the city and enjoy outdoor events and festivals.

Brisbane & Cairns: Expect warmer temperatures of 64°F (18°C) to 84°F (29°C), ideal for enjoying the natural beauty of the region.

New   Zealand

New Zealand's climate is temperate, with significant variation depending on the region and season. While the weather is often mild, it can change rapidly, especially in coastal areas.

Summer (December to February): Summer is the most popular time to cruise in New Zealand, offering pleasant temperatures and clear skies.

Auckland: Expect temperatures between 63°F (17°C) and 79°F (26°C), making it ideal for outdoor activities, beach visits, and sightseeing.

Wellington: The capital enjoys temperatures between 59°F (15°C) and 72°F (22°C), which are comfortable for walking around and exploring the waterfront.

Queenstown: Summer temperatures range from 59°F (15°C) to 77°F (25°C), ideal for adventure activities like hiking, bungee jumping, and wine tasting.

Autumn (March to May): Autumn is also a great time to visit New Zealand, with moderate temperatures and fewer crowds.

Auckland: Temperatures drop slightly to between 59°F (15°C) and 72°F (22°C), but the weather remains pleasant for sightseeing.

Wellington: Average temperatures range from 52°F (11°C) to 64°F (18°C), making it a great time to enjoy outdoor parks and the local food scene.

Queenstown: Autumn temperatures are mild, ranging from 48°F (9°C) to 63°F

(17°C), offering cool nights and warm days—perfect for nature walks and lake cruises.

Winter (June to August): Winter is the off-season in New Zealand, but it offers a quieter experience with fewer tourists.

Auckland: Winter temperatures range from 46°F (8°C) to 61°F (16°C), which is relatively mild, though it can be rainy.

Wellington: Expect temperatures between 41°F (5°C) and 57°F (14°C), with the possibility of occasional snow on the hills but mild in the city center.

Queenstown: The colder months bring cooler temperatures of 32°F (0°C) to 46°F

(8°C), ideal for skiing, snowboarding, and other winter sports in the nearby mountains.

Spring (September to November): Spring offers warming temperatures and the beauty of flowers in bloom, making it an excellent time to visit.

Auckland: Expect temperatures between 54°F (12°C) and 70°F (21°C), perfect for outdoor excursions and city sightseeing.

Wellington: Spring sees temperatures ranging from 46°F (8°C) to 64°F (18°C), and the city comes alive with festivals and events.

Queenstown: Spring temperatures range from 46°F (8°C) to 64°F (18°C), making it a great time for nature walks and adventure sports.

The weather can have a significant impact on cruise schedules and shore excursions in both Australia and New Zealand. While cruise lines generally have contingency plans for weather disruptions, it's still important to understand how certain conditions can affect your cruise experience.

Storms and Rough Seas

Cyclone Season (November to April): The cyclone season in the tropical regions of Australia and New Zealand, particularly in places like Cairns and Queensland, can bring intense storms and rough seas. If a cyclone warning is issued, cruise itineraries may be altered, or some ports might be skipped to avoid adverse weather conditions. Always check with your cruise line for updates on weather-related changes.

Severe Weather: If heavy rain or winds occur in any of the ports, some excursions may be canceled or altered. For example, water-based activities like snorkeling, kayaking, or boat tours may be temporarily suspended for safety reasons.

Temperature Extremes

Hot Weather: In regions like Brisbane and Cairns, temperatures during the summer months can be sweltering, potentially leading to heat advisories. This may affect shore excursions like walking tours, hiking, or outdoor activities, especially in exposed areas like the Outback. On such days, it's important to stay hydrated, wear sunscreen, and seek shade as much as possible.

Cold Weather: In New Zealand, particularly in the southern regions like Queenstown, winter temperatures can be cold and snowy. This weather is perfect for winter sports enthusiasts but might affect outdoor activities like hiking, sightseeing, or boat tours on the lakes.

Rain and Humidity

Rainy Season in Tropical Regions: While tropical regions like Cairns and the

Whitsundays offer great weather for most of the year, the rainy season (November to March) can bring heavy showers and high humidity. This may lead to canceled excursions like beach visits or rainforest tours. Plan for rain by packing waterproof clothing and checking the weather forecast.

Rain in New Zealand: New Zealand's weather can be unpredictable, with rain common year-round. However, the rain often adds to the beauty of places like Fiordland National Park, where the waterfalls are particularly stunning after a rainfall. Always carry an umbrella or a waterproof jacket when exploring the country's coastal or forested regions.

The best time to cruise Australia and New Zealand largely depends on your weather preferences and the type of activities you want to enjoy.

Australia

Best Time to Cruise: November to March (summer) is the ideal time for cruising in Australia, offering warm weather and great conditions for outdoor activities, beach visits, and sightseeing.

Avoid: June to August (winter) if you prefer warmer weather, as temperatures are cooler in southern regions like Melbourne and Sydney.

New Zealand

Best Time to Cruise: **December to February** (summer) offers the best weather for outdoor excursions, with mild temperatures and plenty of sunshine.

Avoid: **May to August** (winter) if you're not a fan of colder temperatures, although winter sports enthusiasts may prefer this time for skiing and snowboarding.

CHAPTER 9: TIPS FOR FIRST-TIME CRUISERS IN AUSTRALIA & NEW ZEALAND

Cruising to Australia and New Zealand offers an incredible way to explore these two stunning destinations, but if it's your first time cruising, there are a few things to keep in mind to ensure you get the most out of your experience. From essential pre-cruise preparations to understanding the local tipping culture and safety tips for families and solo travelers, this chapter will provide all the advice you need to make your first cruise an unforgettable one.

For first-time cruisers, the experience can be exciting but overwhelming. Knowing a few basics before you board your cruise ship can help reduce stress and ensure a smooth start to your journey.

Booking and Pre-Cruise Essentials

Choose the Right Cruise Line: Different cruise lines cater to different types of travelers. If you're a first-time cruiser, look for a cruise line that's known for its ease of access and welcoming atmosphere. Major lines like Carnival, Royal Caribbean, and Princess are well-suited for beginners, offering plenty of guidance and easy-to-navigate experiences.

Documentation and Travel Insurance: Ensure you have all your travel documents ready, including your passport, any necessary visas, and boarding passes. Travel insurance is also highly recommended for peace of mind in case of unexpected cancellations, health issues, or other emergencies.

Check-in Process: Arriving early at the port will give you ample time for check-in, security screening, and boarding. Cruise terminals can sometimes be crowded, so it's advisable to get there at least 2-3 hours before your scheduled departure.

Packing for Your Cruise

Essential Items: Pack the basics, including comfortable clothing for excursions, formal attire for any gala dinners or specialty restaurant nights, swimwear, sunscreen, and a camera for capturing the beautiful scenery.

Layered Clothing: While the weather in Australia and New Zealand is generally mild, temperatures can vary between ports. Packing layers ensures you're prepared for changes in the weather, especially during shore excursions.

Packing for Shore Excursions: If you plan to visit beaches, national parks, or do any outdoor activities, remember to pack water shoes, comfortable walking shoes, hats, and insect repellent.

Embarkation Day Tips

Arrive Early: Arriving early helps you get settled and familiar with the ship. It's also helpful in case there are delays or queues. Once on board, you'll usually have access to the main dining areas and other common areas, so you can start enjoying your cruise as soon as possible.

Ship Tour: Take some time to explore the ship on embarkation day. Cruise lines often offer guided tours of the ship to familiarize passengers with all its facilities, including dining rooms, pools, spas, and entertainment areas.

Handling money while cruising is something many first-time travelers need to get used to. Knowing the currency, tipping norms, and budget-friendly options can help you avoid unnecessary confusion or surprises.

Currency

Australia: The currency in Australia is the Australian Dollar (AUD). Many places in larger cities and popular tourist destinations accept credit cards, but it's still a good idea to carry cash for smaller purchases, tips, or in case you visit remote areas where card payment may not be available.

New Zealand: The currency in New Zealand is the New Zealand Dollar (NZD). Similar to Australia, credit cards are widely accepted, but it's always helpful to have some local cash for convenience, especially in rural areas.

Onboard Currency: Most cruise lines use a cashless payment system on board, where all purchases are charged to your cabin account. You'll typically provide a credit card at check-in, and all on-board spending (drinks, excursions, souvenirs) will be added to your bill. At the end of the cruise, you'll settle your account before disembarking.

Tipping Culture

Australia: Tipping in Australia is not mandatory, and service workers generally don't expect tips. However, rounding up your bill or leaving a small tip for exceptional service (around 10%) is appreciated, especially in high-end restaurants or for guided tours.

New Zealand: Similar to Australia, tipping is not a widespread practice in New Zealand. However, in restaurants or for private tours, you may leave a 10% tip for good service. It's also common to leave small tips for hotel staff or tour guides.

Cruise Tips: On cruises, tips are typically included in the service charges or automatically added to your onboard account (usually around $12–$20 USD per day). If you feel that a specific staff member (like your waiter or room steward) has gone above and beyond, you can always give additional tips directly.

Budget-Friendly Options

Free and Inclusive Dining: While cruises often offer specialty dining options for an additional fee, there are plenty of included dining venues, such as buffets, main dining rooms, and casual eateries. These options offer delicious meals without extra charges.

Excursions: Many cruise lines offer complimentary shore excursions, like city walking tours or beach visits. Alternatively, booking excursions in advance through your cruise line might give you access to discounts and bundle deals.

Onboard Activities: Most cruise activities, such as poolside games, dance classes, and entertainment shows, are free of charge. However, some classes, special events, or access to exclusive areas like spas or fitness centers may come with an additional fee.

Safety Tips for Solo Travelers and Families

Safety should always be a priority, especially for solo travelers and families. Whether you're cruising solo or with loved ones, being aware of safety protocols and tips will ensure that you have a safe and enjoyable cruise experience.

Solo Travelers

Meet Fellow Travelers: Cruises are a great way to meet new people. Solo travelers can join group activities, tours, or even cruise-sponsored meetups designed for solo cruisers. It's a perfect way to bond with others and share experiences.

Stay Connected: While onboard, make sure to stay connected with family or friends back home. Most ships have Wi-Fi, though it may come with additional costs. Many ships also offer phone packages for staying in touch while in port.

Personal Safety: Always keep your cabin door locked when inside, and never open it to strangers. If you're going ashore on your own, let someone know where you're going and what time you plan to return. It's also wise to carry a small, secure bag for personal items and avoid displaying valuables in public areas.

Families with Children

Kids' Clubs: Many cruise lines offer supervised kids' programs, where children can participate in age-appropriate activities and make friends. These programs are perfect for giving parents a break while ensuring kids are safe and entertained.

Safety Onboard: While cruising, ensure that your children are familiar with the ship's safety protocols, such as the location of muster stations (where safety drills take place) and how to access emergency equipment. Always keep an eye on young children around pools or other water activities.

Shore Excursions for Families: Look for family-friendly excursions that cater to younger children or those with less mobility. Tours with nature walks, wildlife spotting, or visits to family-friendly beaches are often great options for families with kids.

General Safety Tips for All Passengers

Emergency Preparedness: Familiarize yourself with the ship's emergency procedures and locations of lifeboats and life jackets. Every cruise will conduct a mandatory safety drill on embarkation day, so make sure you attend and listen carefully.

Health Precautions: Keep your health in mind while onboard and in port. If you're prone to seasickness, it's advisable to take seasickness medication before you board. On land, be cautious with food and water, especially if you're in more remote areas of Australia or New Zealand.

CHAPTER 10: HEALTH AND WELLNESS ONBOARD AND ONSHORE

Embarking on a cruise to Australia and New Zealand presents not only the chance to explore vibrant cities and stunning landscapes but also an opportunity to maintain your health and wellness while on vacation. Whether you're looking to stay fit while at sea, indulge in luxurious wellness services, or prioritize safety during your onshore excursions, this chapter provides tips and insights to help you stay in top shape throughout your cruise.

Cruising doesn't have to mean abandoning your health goals. Onboard cruise ships, you'll find plenty of options for staying active and maintaining a healthy lifestyle during your vacation. Here's how you can stay fit and healthy while cruising:

Take Advantage of the Fitness Center
Most cruise ships feature state-of-the-art fitness centers with a wide range of equipment, from treadmills and ellipticals to free weights and resistance machines. These facilities offer a great opportunity to maintain your workout routine while enjoying the breathtaking views of the ocean.

Cardio and Strength Workouts: Whether you prefer high-intensity cardio workouts or strength training, the gym on your cruise ship will have a variety of machines and free weights to help you stay in shape.

Personal Training Sessions: Many cruise lines offer personal training sessions at an additional cost. These personalized sessions are a great option for those looking for tailored fitness routines or expert advice while on board.

Participate in Fitness Classes

In addition to gym equipment, most cruise ships offer a variety of fitness classes that you can join throughout the day. These classes are typically included in the cruise package, but some specialty classes (such as yoga or spinning) may come with an extra fee.

Yoga and Pilates: Yoga and Pilates classes are available to help you stretch, relax, and strengthen your core. These classes often take place in scenic areas of the ship, such as on the top deck with an ocean view.

Aerobics and Dance: Many cruise ships offer group aerobics classes, Zumba, or dance classes, which are not only fun but also great for cardio and toning.

Water Aerobics: For a low-impact workout, water aerobics classes in the ship's pool are an excellent way to stay active without putting strain on your joints.

Explore the Decks and Walkways

Take a stroll around the deck or explore the ship's walking paths to get some exercise while enjoying the sea breeze. Walking is an easy and relaxing way to stay active while enjoying the surroundings. Many cruise ships feature walking tracks on their upper decks, where you can walk laps and enjoy the view.

Outdoor Sports and Activities

Cruise ships often have outdoor sports facilities such as basketball courts, mini-golf, tennis courts, or even rock-climbing walls. These activities are perfect for anyone who wants to stay active while having fun. If you enjoy outdoor activities, be sure to check out what's available on your ship.

Healthy Eating Options

Maintaining a healthy diet while cruising can be just as important as staying physically active. Many cruise ships offer healthier menu options, including low-calorie, low-fat, and vegetarian dishes. You can ask the staff for suggestions, and most cruise lines are happy to accommodate dietary preferences like gluten-free, vegan, or low-sodium diets.

Smaller Portions: Many cruise lines will allow you to order smaller portions if you're looking to keep your meals balanced. Avoid overindulging, especially at buffets, and focus on eating a variety of nutrient-rich foods.

Hydrate: Staying hydrated is crucial, especially when spending time in warmer climates like Australia and New Zealand. Always carry a water bottle and avoid sugary drinks, which can lead to dehydration.

Top Wellness Services Available on Cruise Ships

Cruise ships are not only about dining, entertainment, and excursions; they also offer an array of wellness services to help you relax, rejuvenate, and refresh. Whether you're looking for a spa treatment, a relaxing massage, or a rejuvenating beauty treatment, here's what you can expect to find on board:

Spa   Treatments

Most cruise lines have luxurious onboard spas offering a wide range of treatments. You can book a spa day or select individual treatments to help you unwind and pamper yourself during your cruise.

Massages: From Swedish massages to hot stone massages, cruise ship spas offer various types of massages to relieve stress and improve circulation.

Facials: Revitalize your skin with a soothing facial, tailored to your skin type. Many spas offer rejuvenating treatments to combat the effects of sun exposure or air travel.

Body Scrubs and Wraps: Treat yourself to a hydrating body scrub or wrap to exfoliate and nourish your skin, leaving it feeling soft and refreshed.

Wellness and Relaxation Programs
Beyond traditional spa treatments, many cruise ships offer wellness and relaxation programs aimed at improving both your physical and mental well-being.

Meditation and Mindfulness: Some cruise lines offer meditation classes or relaxation sessions to help you clear your mind and reduce stress.

Saunas and Steam Rooms: Most cruise ships have saunas and steam rooms, ideal for relaxing after a long day of sightseeing or workouts. These facilities promote detoxification and muscle relaxation.

Thermal Suites: Some ships offer luxury thermal suites, which combine heat therapy with water-based treatments to promote relaxation and rejuvenation.

Fitness and Yoga Retreats For those seeking a more immersive wellness experience, many cruise lines offer fitness or yoga retreats during the voyage. These retreats often include fitness classes, yoga sessions, and nutrition workshops, all designed to help you reset and recharge.

Wellness Packages: These all-inclusive packages offer a range of wellness services, including fitness classes, healthy eating tips, and access to spa treatments. They're perfect for travelers who want a more dedicated wellness experience during their cruise.

Beauty and Hair Care Services Cruise ship salons offer a wide array of beauty treatments and hair care services, from hairstyling and haircuts to manicures and pedicures. Treat yourself to a beauty session and feel pampered throughout your trip.

Manicures and Pedicures: Cruise ship salons often offer luxurious manicures and pedicures with a variety of nail treatments, including gel polish, nail art, and foot massages.

Hair Styling: Whether you want a fresh haircut or a stunning blowout, cruise ship salons provide professional hair services that'll leave you looking your best for formal nights or excursions.

Staying Safe During Excursions, Including Water Activities

Staying safe during shore excursions, especially water-based activities, is essential to ensure a fun and secure experience while exploring Australia and New Zealand. Follow these safety tips to help you enjoy your adventures both onboard and onshore.

Follow Safety Instructions and Guidelines

Whether you're on a guided tour, exploring the Great Barrier Reef, or kayaking in

Rotorua's lakes, always listen to the instructions provided by your guide or crew members. Safety briefings are crucial and ensure that you understand the risks and how to minimize them.

Life Jackets: For water-based activities such as kayaking, snorkeling, or boating, always wear a life jacket, even if you're an experienced swimmer. It's a simple safety precaution that can save your life in case of an emergency.

Guided Tours: Opt for guided shore excursions with reputable tour operators. These operators are well-versed in safety procedures and provide well-maintained equipment for activities like diving, rafting, or wildlife safaris.

Know   Your   Limits
While adventurous activities like hiking, diving, and water sports can be exhilarating, it's important to recognize your own physical limits. If you're unsure about your ability to handle a particular activity, don't hesitate to speak up and choose a more suitable alternative.

Snorkeling and Diving: If you've never snorkeled or dived before, start with beginner-friendly excursions, where guides provide clear instructions and assistance. Instructors will guide you step-by-step to ensure your safety.

Hiking and Walking Tours: Some excursions involve challenging terrain, so make sure you choose tours that are appropriate for your fitness level. Always wear suitable footwear and take necessary precautions against sun exposure and dehydration.

Protect Yourself from the Sun
Australia and New Zealand have some of the highest levels of UV radiation in the world, so protecting yourself from the sun is essential to prevent sunburn and other skin damage.

Sunscreen: Always apply sunscreen with a high SPF, especially when you're engaging in outdoor activities like hiking, walking tours, or water sports. Reapply sunscreen every 2-3 hours, or more frequently if swimming.

Hats and Sunglasses: Wear a wide-brimmed hat and UV-protection sunglasses to shield your eyes and face from the sun. This helps to reduce the risk of heatstroke and protects sensitive skin from UV damage.

Be Mindful of Water Conditions
Before engaging in any water activity, such as swimming, kayaking, or snorkeling, make sure you're aware of the water conditions.

Currents and Tides: Some beaches and water areas, especially along the coastlines of Australia and New Zealand, can have strong currents or unpredictable tides. Always follow the advice of local guides, and don't swim in areas where swimming is prohibited.

Water Quality: Ensure that the water quality in certain areas is safe for swimming. Some regions may have jellyfish, strong currents, or other hazards that could impact your safety. In such cases, it's always wise to use protective clothing like a stinger suit or follow safety guidelines.

CONCLUSION: YOUR PERFECT AUSTRALIA & NEW ZEALAND CRUISE AWAITS

As you reach the end of this guide, it's clear that your upcoming cruise to Australia and New Zealand is set to be nothing short of an adventure of a lifetime. From the iconic landmarks like the Sydney Opera House and the Great Barrier Reef to the breathtaking landscapes of New Zealand's Fiordland and Rotorua's geothermal wonders, these two countries offer an incredible mix of natural beauty, vibrant cities, and rich cultural experiences.

This is your opportunity to experience the wonders of the Southern Hemisphere in a way that few other types of vacations can offer. Imagine waking up each morning to stunning ocean views, knowing that every day brings a new adventure—whether you're exploring bustling cities, relaxing on pristine beaches, or immersing yourself in the fascinating cultures of these two remarkable nations.

But before you embark on your journey, remember that careful planning is key to making the most of your time on board and ashore. From choosing the right cruise line to understanding the best time to visit, your journey begins long before you step foot on the ship. Take the time to choose a cruise that fits your interests and preferences, whether you want to relax and unwind or embark on a more adventurous itinerary.

Choose the Right Cruise Line for Your Needs

Whether you're looking for luxury, family-friendly fun, or a more laid-back cruising experience, there are a variety of cruise lines that cater to different types of travelers. Research your options and look for one that aligns with your vacation style, whether it's a relaxed, all-inclusive voyage or one with more active and immersive excursions.

Plan Your Shore Excursions

Research the shore excursions available at each port. If you're into nature, look for

182

tours that highlight the country's wildlife and landscapes. If you love history and culture, seek out local tours that delve into the rich heritage of the areas you'll be visiting.

Check for Special Deals and Packages
Cruises to Australia and New Zealand can be expensive, but there are often deals or packages that can help save money. Look for early bird discounts, group deals, or package deals that combine cruise and shore excursions to get the best value for your money.

Timing   Is   Everything
As we discussed, the best time to cruise varies depending on your preferences. If you

prefer warmer weather and long days, cruising during the Australian summer (November to March) is ideal. However, if you want to avoid large crowds, the autumn or spring months can also offer a great experience with milder weather.

Book Early to Secure Your Spot

Australia and New Zealand cruises are very popular, especially during peak seasons, so it's a good idea to book early to secure the best cabins and your desired departure date. By booking early, you'll also have the opportunity to make reservations for shore excursions, specialty dining, and spa treatments in advance, ensuring a smoother experience.

Embrace the Adventure

Now that you have all the information you need, it's time to take the next step and start planning the cruise that will bring you to the shores of two of the most incredible destinations on Earth. Australia and New Zealand offer a wealth of experiences—from vibrant cities and cultural heritage to natural wonders that will leave you speechless. Whether you're traveling solo, as a couple, or with family, there's something for everyone on this unforgettable journey.

So, don't wait any longer—your perfect Australia & New Zealand cruise awaits. Start planning, book the right cruise, and get ready for the trip of a lifetime. The adventure you've been dreaming of is just around the corner!

Made in the USA
Monee, IL
25 July 2025

21908074R00105